Memories at the End of the Line

Brianna Bailey

BookLeaf Publishing

India | USA | UK

Presentation by *BookLeaf Publishing*

Web: www.bookleafpub.com

E-mail: info@bookleafpub.com

ISBN: 9789360940874

First edition 2024

To my family and friends, thank you for encouraging me to take this leap of faith.

Opening Up

Are you ready to begin now?

What am I here for?

Relax, Ms. Jones.

Eyes on the exit.
Watch the door.
Close it, lock it,
Just like before.

Let's talk about your childhood.

A world I can't remember anymore.

This is a safe space.

I've heard that lie before.
There's no such thing as safety.
Not for me.
Not for years.
If I close my eyes, I can disappear.

Let's talk about August 3rd.
Why did you feel the need to run?

The world is black and wet with tears.
Running keeps you safe from haunting fears.
Don't want to go back to that old train line,
But feel the mind go back in time

Take a breath,
Let's go back to the beginning.

There's no escaping.

Fairytale

At age six, I dreamt of fairy tales,
A marble castle from ceiling to floor.
I'd line up all my dolls, my maidens,
And waltz right through my bedroom door.
For I am the queen of all I see.
And for as long as I will reign,
Long live Queen Angel!
They will cheer,
And sing praises to my name.

At ten, I dreamt of fairy tales,
Of a true love I'd yet to meet.
I'd fantasize about deep brown eyes,
Then, switch them to emerald green.
I'd swoon at how his voice would sound.
A rich, velvet baritone,
With words of love for me alone.
He'd call me Darling no-
He'd say Love.
He'd call me Angel, sent from above.

I used to dream of fairy tales.
Then, at sixteen, my dreams came true.
Monty, my prince, arrived in June.
A blooming romance at long last.

His brown eyes matched my fantasy.
His voice was smooth and deep.
If only I had heard the honeyed lies,
In between the words, he'd speak.
Oh, but love is blind and deaf,
And the joke was all on me.

I used to dream of fairy tales.
Now, at thirty,
I no longer sleep.

End of the Line

He took me to the Greyhound at night on August
3rd.
Two one-way tickets to the end of the line.

Eighteen years old and still in love with a
fantasy.
Like Romeo and Juliet, we were star-crossed
lovers,
I should have known there would be no happy
ending.

Like a moth to a flame, I followed to the end of
the line.
And the world I left behind burned to ash.

Date Night

Spin me 'round the dance floor.
Hear the bass and groove.
Whisper in my ear, I'm yours.
Hear my heartbeat boom boom boom.

Lights and rhythm intertwine,
Burn my throat with liquid sin.
Hands of strangers grab and hold.
Twist and move and-
Boom, boom, boom
Hear the green-eyed thunder roar.

Pull me 'round and 'round the dance floor.
Whisper in my ear I'm yours.

Only yours.

Puppet Master

Baby, promise that you trust me?
Trust and never question.
Baby, promise that you love me?
Suffocate in my affection.

Baby, promise that you need me?
I'll break you till you know.
Promise you won't leave me.
There's nowhere else to go.

You know you make me crazy,
And I just want you safe.
Be a good girl and obey me,
'Cause I'll never let you leave.

You know you can't go out like that.
Put a smile on your face.
My money bought your hopes and dreams.
You will do as I say.

Let me hold you closer.
I want you always in my space.
Baby, say you love me.
'Cause you'll never walk away.

Burning Love

Warm like the sunlight.
Golden rays kiss upon the skin.
A heated blanket for the coldest nights.
Like the flames of a firepit,
Embrace the smoke and smile.
Ignore the cinder and ash,
This flame holds something sweet.
Rise, golden blaze, and conspire.
Punish the unattentive Icarus.
Turn smoke into shackles.
Let the flames bite and burrow inside.
Past the ribs and lungs, it penetrates.
Target acquired.

Love Me, Love Me Not

Watch the snow-white petals fall,
Wrapped in bliss and security.
Provide and protect his lady love,
He loves me.

Hear the snarling wolf awake.
Look what I make him do to me,
But tomorrow will be a better day.
He loves me.

Taste the bittersweet candied berries.
Apologize and reassure.
Kiss and wipe away my anxious tears.
He loves me.

Feel the cool air dance on my skin.
The joy and freedom of independence.
Stumble, laugh, and tell the world,
He loves me.

Past the witching hour now,
Smell the whiskey on his breath.
Feel the shattered glass and heart.
Taste crimson copper and salted tears.
Hear the howl and realize,

The mask has fallen.
Watch him walk away from his broken-record
toy.

He loves me.
He loves me.
He loves me,
Not.

Dear Love

To The Man Who Claimed to Love Me,
Thank you for opening my eyes.
The facade is gone from your expression;
 I see the darkness you hide.
No more having to surrender.
No more sweaters worn in June.
No more tears across the bedsheets.
No more lies; I'll hear from you.
Hope this letter finds you well, dear.
 Hope you choke upon your yells.
Wishing you the best, babe.
As you go straight down to Hell.
You fix me only to break me.
You say loving me ain't cheap?
Return all of the love you bought.
I can love myself for free.

Runaway

Midnight train to anywhere.
A one-way ticket's all I need.
I've run from home for long enough.
To the end of the line,
Godspeed.
There's a storm I left behind me,
And in front, a ray of hope.
Midnight train,
To the end of the line.
Midnight train,
To home.

Home Again

Daddy's working in his office.
Mama's got dinner on the stove.
The neighbors watch and stare in awe,
Cause look how much you've grown.
You'll be the gossip of the town.
There's too much they'll want to know.
But pray the door will open and hear,
Baby, welcome home.

Walk with caution, hope, and tremble.
But there are words you have to say.
How many sorries in a lifetime?
Cause it's not enough for just one day.
Will Daddy take you by the hand?
Will Mama hug you tight?
As the guilt takes over, beg to hear,
Baby, it's alright.

If you could turn back time today,
If you knew then what you know now…
But make the bed and lie in it.
You played the game of love and war,
And lost until you quit.
But baby, it's okay,
Cause the game has now reset.

Down the faded pastel sidewalk,
There's the rustling of the wind.
And it gives you clear instructions,
To where you've gone and where you've been.
The sun sets all around you,
Baby, hurry cause the night is setting in.

See them on the porch ahead.
Illuminated by its glow
Almost there.
Getting closer.
Ignore the shadows creeping up.
Block out wind's decrees.
One step ahead.
Just keep running.
Both their arms are opened wide.
Then, hear the wind call,
Baby, open your eyes.

And just like that, you're back again,
Under tenacious lock and key.
A goodbye letter on the floor.
And when you look up to meet the warden's gaze,
You see the gates of Hell to pay.
And there's no money high enough to fit his price.
But the highest currency he deems,
Is life.

Friends and Spirits

Flashing lights and spinning haze.
Fly me to the galaxy.
Spirits high and friends all around.
Jack and Jim will cut a rug.
Brandy will laugh at nothing and everything.
Loose lip Stella tells the truth.
With friends like these who cares for problems?
Over the lips and through the gums.
Another round bartender!
I still remember everything.

What's In A Name?

My parents named me Angel,
Princess worked just fine.
But if they called me Angel Lynn,
There was trouble on the line.

The neighbors called me Angie.
My cousins called me Sis.
My school friends called me Jonesy,
But I was glad that didn't stick.

My PawPaw called me Kiddo,
And Nana called me Sweets.
Though Uncle Kevin, hard of hearing,
Would swear my name was Sheets.

I've had so many names in life,
But I never would've thought.
I'd get a name on Thursday night,
From a stick and bathroom stall.

Bad Joke

Knock, knock,
Who's there?
Not you, not you.
You don't exist here.
I know it's not true.
Knock, knock,
Who's there?
Not you, not you.
You'll be gone by morning.
When I wake up in my room.
Knock, knock,
Who's there?
Doesn't matter,
This is all make-believe.
Knock, knock,
There's nobody home.
Knock, knock,
Please leave me alone.
Knock, knock,
I can't let you in.
This can't be real,
It has to be all pretend.
I only imagined two lines at the end.

Aftermath

We got a happy ending.
Close the book,
The story's done.
Pay no mind to Mother, dear,
It's just hormones overrun.
Finally, with bated breath, our family is
complete.
Adding to splintered branches on the family tree.

I've wanted this since I was young.
I imagined who they'd be.
Their father's eyes.
My hair and nose.
A child combines the best parts,
Of you and me.

So why, when I think about it,
Does my stomach knot with dread?
A tiny human, sweet and pure,
Makes me terrified.
Then I see you looming over me,
When I think about its eyes.
And when a tiny hand appears,
I feel yours at my sides.
I feel them wrapped around my throat,

And my heart breaks in two,
Because I know this baby made
Came with no love from you.

Innocent new life has begun,
From guilty acts of sin.
The tears were shed,
The deed is done,
But I-
I can't let him win.

Shifting Minds

Ms. Jones, welcome back.
I can sense there's been a shift since our last
talk.

For the first time, she'll see a smile.
Shifting, now I haven't done that in a while.

Then, let's talk about that in today's session.
What would you say was the biggest shift in
your life?

Aside from the August 3rd train ride?
I lived drunk, scared, and foolish.
Let that man in my life.
Lived each day with regrets and anxiety of strife.
But,
I remember the day when it all turned around.

Shall we begin?

This time, I'm ready.

What If?

Regrets in life are common.
God knows I've had a few.
So many things you wished you'd said.
So many people you wished you'd seen.
I've lived my life around What-If,
Should've, Could've, Would've been.

What if I didn't skip school that day?
I would have climbed the rope in gym.
Had an invite to Jenna's party,
Passed a Spanish quiz…I think.
Instead, I skipped for the mall and movies.
A rebellious phase, I guess.
And it brought me down this foolish road,
This never would've happened in Math.

I should've called my parents to tell them I was
safe.
What if we had stayed in touch?
They would have pulled me off the train.
Mama would have told me love would come
soon.
Daddy would've said I was too young,
But there went the stupid argument.
If you don't like our rules, don't live here at all!

And I wish I had listened way back then.
I wish I had apologized.

I want to go back home one day,
To make what-ifs a dream come true.
No more regrets and no more pain.
At least I'd get a second chance,
But as I'm sitting at the bartop,
Pondering all that could've been.
I think about the future,
And I wonder who you'll be.

Crossroads

Where do you go at the end of the crossroads?
What do you do when no path seems right?
There's a dark path, on the one hand,
But I've walked it once before.
A smoke and fog so thick and dense,
Feels like it's clawing at your throat.

The ground is made of roses, but the beauty is
skin deep.
And by the time you realize,
The thorn cuts are sharp and deep.
I looked down at the other end,
The length's about the same,
And while it looks well-kept and lit,
Shadows are lurking in the shade.
I know there are other options, but morals never
sway.
There's no one I know well enough to take this
fear away.
So I'm stuck here at the crossroads for another
day.

I came back to the crossroads.
Looked at both paths, old and new.
On one hand, I could see the sun,

Would I even like the view?
However, if I stuck with what I knew,
I wouldn't feel alone.
I'd have my life I spent with you,
But could that be a home?
So here I stand,
Still at the crossroads,
Wondering which way to go.

Here's to two months at the crossroads,
But now my choice is clear.
I'll walk the shaded path with hesitation,
But not fear.
I'm not sure what awaits me.
I don't know what's wrong or right.
But I heard the beat of an angel's wing,
And I know it changed my life.

Angels don't belong in darkness.
How ironic it is to say.
But if I go right at the crossroads,
Then, at least, I'll see the sun.
I'll protect this little heartbeat.
My sweet baby,
We are one.

Playtime's Over

Once upon a time, you told me I was yours.
I didn't fight it then.
I just let you take control.
Convinced myself that this was how you loved.
I didn't protest when you grabbed me
I gave up when you screamed
Everything was my fault
That's how I knew it'd always be

You wanted so much to break me.
Remind me that I was just a toy.
You never thought you'd give me a tiny ray of
hope.
Baby, we're a family, yet you never seem to stay.
Isn't this what you wanted?
This means you won our game.
Or is it finally getting through to you,
Things will never be the same.

Mother vs. Mother

In the middle of a hurricane, there's a calming peace.
But you don't forget the crashing rains.
Demolished homes and cries of grief.
But the eye is a trickster cloaked in leaves.
Mother Nature's touch is gentle,
And she leaves you space to think.
But only in the eye can you feel it's safe to breathe.

As it passes overhead, the blue sky fades to black.
The thunder taunts and jeers at you.
It tells you welcome back.
Implore dear Mother Nature to let you stop and rest.
But with a crack of lightning, hear,
Mother always knows best.

The instincts meant to run and hide,
Now scream out to protect what lives inside.
When the angered wind comes howling,
When the thunder rocks, the quiet,
When the rain above us crashes,
And the whips of lightning flashes.

I'll brace myself for every strike,
And hold the home's foundation tight.
If life's the hurricane outside,
I'll keep you safe inside the eye

The Good Ending

The most beautiful things in the world aren't
free.
There's always been a price.
Some people pay with money; some may use
their time.
Then there are the priceless gifts,
Like bringing in new life.

I thought I had been through hell and back,
Except this takes the cake.
I can feel my body shake and tremble with the
pain.
Although, despite what I feel now,
There's still everything to gain.

I need one last push, so I'll give it all I've got.
One more time, the nurses say.
One scream, and then I hear the softest little
waa.
The most precious sound I've ever heard,
The pain before is left forgotten.

In the room now, it's just you and me.
Small little bundle all wrapped in pink.
I wish I could tell you that life won't be hard.

I'll try to shield you from all mommy's scars.
Baby girl, as I hold you close, always know,
As long as I live,
You won't ever feel alone.

www.ingramcontent.com/pod-product-compliance
Lightning Source LLC
LaVergne TN
LVHW021342200726
843509LV00014B/2626